Flatback Sally Country

Also by Rachel Custer

The Temple She Became

Flatback Sally Country

Rachel Custer

Terrapin Books

© 2023 by Rachel Custer
Printed in the United States of America.
All rights reserved.
No part of this book may be reproduced in any manner, except for brief quotations embodied in critical articles or reviews.

Terrapin Books
4 Midvale Avenue
West Caldwell, NJ 07006

www.terrapinbooks.com

ISBN: 978-1-947896-62-8
Library of Congress Control Number: 2022948282

First Edition

Cover art: Evan Stuart Marshall
Leaving Home, 2019
acrylic on canvas, 20 x 20 inches
© Evan Stuart Marshall

Cover Design: Diane Lockward

for Deb and Jaqlyn, always

Contents

History   3

One
Boat   7
Property   8
The Whole Town Knows Sally Is a Slut   9
Bait   10
Look   12
Fire   13
Listen, Baby   14
The Old Man Warns
   the Young Man at the Bar   15
Type   16
Drive   18
Sally Considers Taking the Train Away   19
House Soon to Catch Fire   20

Two
Song   25
Stripper   26
Magical Thinking   27
Sinners Anonymous   28
Birthright   29
Mother   30
Park   31
Woman   33
Knock Knock   34
Grandmother   35
Sally Teaches Mercy Best She Knows   36
Daughter   37

Three

Shadows	41
Crank	42
That Saved a Wretch Like Me	43
Emigrant	44
Field	46
Factory	47
Lines Written Between Shifts	48
Settlement	49
House Down in the Holler	50
The End of the Eggs	51
Work Song of the Unbroken, Joyfully	52
Consider the Trigger	54
Tommy Two Fingers Quits His Job	55
Even the Road Away Leads Sally Home	56

Four

Mercy, Defined	59
Kid	60
Farmer	62
Boy	64
Wanderer	65
Old Maid	66
Preacher	67
Liquor Store Clerk	69
The Grand Dragon of the KKK Is Buried Near My House	70
Soldier	72
Seeing Too Much Is Seeing Nothing	73
As for me and my house, we will	74

Acknowledgments	77
About the Author	79

Where you come from is gone, where you thought you were going to never was there, and where you are is no good unless you can get away from it.

—Flannery O'Connor, *Wise Blood*

History

There is only one story a woman says and maybe
she is saying something about the truth, or maybe
not. The history of a place like this is the history
of those who leave it. It's a great place to be *from*
they might say, and smile. Pretty men and pretty
women and their easy belief that they are moving
forward through the world. Their necks graceful
in their city clothes. *There is only one story* and
it is not this story, sweat and grease and the grace
of ritualized days. The pinch of repetition in the
joints. The world would be forgiven for believing
the best of this land is the dust that a hand knocks
from old boots. Maybe there is something of the
truth to what she says, like there is only one way
to live in a place one cannot leave, and that's
to love it. Take the raw animal of its days by the
throat and throttle the one story from its jaws. Or
maybe not. There is only one way to live in a place
where everybody believes nobody lives. Like
there is only one way to be a fire and that is to burn.

One

Boat

All day the sky is a closed fist. All day the maple leaves
upraise their silver palms. All day the pregnant air. The dust
and heat. *Meet me out behind my mom's school bus* says one
seventeen-year-old to another, and *I need a cigarette.
I hate this place I can't wait to get out of here.* She kicks
at the gravel, toes a pacifier half-buried in the dirt. It's
the kind of day. *Meet me out behind the smoke shack*
says one eighteen-year-old to another. *As soon as we punch out
for break. I hate this place. I can't wait to get out of here.*
It's the kind of day that hangs. Women move like figureheads,
leaning always into the next thing, gentling through the silence
like low boats. *Just whatta ya think yer laughin' at*
is the most desperate thing ever said by a woman whose belly
hangs from under her shirt. Whose children have never
stopped touching her. It's the kind of day that crouches low
behind your fear. A man slouches slow like a garbage
barge. All day the water main waits beneath the house.
Here is one church for the people who admit they are good
and one church for the people who won't. Their crosses
like identical sinking prows. All day the sky draws back
its fist like a punch is coming and the loud machines pound
between cigarettes. *Meet me outside* says one preacher
to the other preacher. *I hate this place. I can't wait to get out of here.*

Property

She had a man. They lived alone behind
the turned back of the world. They lived
alone around the edge of things. Rooted
their muffled way through long days. He
called her *baby* and sometimes *come here*
and sometimes *you stupid bitch*. His smile
a canyon filled with small bones. The cold
world was her old man in the cold shade
of his old grave whispering *darlin', dance
with the one that brung ya*. Move in the shoes
that first rawed your heels. Nothing
fills silence like a dead father's voice. Or
a single rifle crack. She had a man. She
lived alone. Danced alone in the long shade
of his fear. They dug their way through life.
Baby, he told her, and he bared his teeth
at the air next to her eyes. *If I ever catch you
with another man.* He smiled like her father
when she caught him slipping his hand
up another woman's Sunday dress.
The theater of his teeth. She had a man.
Baby, he said, and her need for him was
a constant atonement of hands. His body
the earth.　　　　　　Her life a tunneling.

The Whole Town Knows Sally Is a Slut

That Mardi Gras of men trampling her
glads, that front porch boot-stomped muddy—
(*buddy, let me tell ya, she's a wildcat, don't
ask me how I know*)—anyway, everybody
male and able-bodied and old enough to drink
knows *that*. Don't look at me like you never
watched her walk away, that sway in them hips,
that quick look back, her lickin' them lips?
The whole town knows what Sally wants.
Hot factory of a woman wants a lunch break
man. A potatoes-and-steak man. I know, I know;
she's a church girl now—on Sunday morning,
what's that mean? Flatback Sally, her nickname's
always been, ever since before she was sixteen.
She was that poor young teacher's dream.
Her practically grown, and more than ready,
and him run out of town for that one thing?
Anyway, Sally. Think I might give her a ring.

Bait

Here's a girl, hefted onto this barbed hook
of a place. Here a girl impaled on a day.
Her fourteen-year-old face raised as if toward
the sun, pink around the writhe of her eyes.
*An earthworm is nothing but skin and the dirt
through which it tunnels,* her father tells her
as he baits his hook. *Don't fool yourself that
he can feel like you.* A girl is made of skin
and the air through which she moves and all
the things her daddy always said. If a hook
can be a home, she has been waiting long
for the cold plunge of metal through her guts.
Has believed it will feel something like love,
or a man. Her pinned, wriggling beneath him
and his strength to provide, his callouses,
his need to make nobody need. If a man
can be a hook, a girl can be two homes:
the dirt he holds and the dirt that buries him.
*A man is nothing but skin and the soil
he calls home,* her mother says, catching her
glance at a man. *Don't fool yourself that he
can feel like you.* A mother is nothing
but skin and the fear through which she tunnels,
and the honesty to call it love. A daughter's
young face rising toward a man. Skin smooth
in his rough light. Her daddy always said,
Go on, girl, fish or cut bait. Dinner won't wait

forever. Small waves against the boat. Brief
pause of her held breath. Brief panic of her
                    hands. Her eyes. Her eyes.

Look

What things half-buried in the dirt of this yard: a hard candy, a used bandaid, the black half-marble of a doll's eye. Like something caged staring back at something free. Like the rest of the doll is down there watching with envy any face that's up here looking down. Dark ground, dark lashes like a little girl's—something here lies that doesn't love the world. Something that glares up at the lifelong march of safety shoes, the trudge to work and back again, and that sees liberty. Its desire only for the room to pace.

                         What things half-buried in the air of this town, desperate faces mooning upward in the night. Like something caged staring back at something free. A hard woman, a used man, the new half-smile of a boy newly in love. Thick summer air that warms what it chokes, and chokes what it warms. The locked cage of a lover's arms. And above us, the cool prison of the Lord's regard. What to call this, the hatred of the earth-bound for the sky? Us socketed to earth like a sightless eye. What to call the expression on the face above? When it is so vast, and we so small? Disinterest and love look the same in the eyes of a doll.

Fire

Halfway down a country road a house leans
as if asking for forgiveness. As if asking
to be remembered well. Remembers the time
the roof caved in after a wet snow and how
the candles made stories of the walls. Nobody
knows hunger like a cold child. Hunger eats
anything it can get, and if hunger gets nothing,
it will eat the house that holds it and make
a dessert of itself. Hunger would rather reign
than serve. *I would rather ask forgiveness
than permission* says a woman, and this woman
knows the truth: how once invited inside,
hunger never leaves. Hunkers in the corner
and glares. It feeds and feeds. A house
leans like a fire waiting to happen. Says a child:
I would rather steal than ask for anything
just before asking a neighbor to borrow
an egg. A man walks to work as if asking
forgiveness, leaning like a house against
the wind. A house could be forgiven for taking
hunger's side, for demanding so much,
for its quiet and constant need. A man
could be forgiven for striking a match.

Listen, Baby

There's nothing worth fighting over
anymore. No red meat

rots on the counter where you forgot
my hands no longer hover

for what you drop. Your work boots
muddy my floor again,

I swear. Hit me like that
first time God came in, found me

flat on my back in church. Singing
a new song. There's nothing

to love about you, said the Lord,
and He was right, and since

He was the Lord I shut my mouth.
There's nothing to love

about, you said, and since
you weren't the Lord, I lifted

my love and shut your mouth for you.

The Old Man Warns the Young Man at the Bar

Flatback Sally 'come a whole new woman
once that sun go down. Run over this little town
just like a glance. Careful, boy, she might
just fall on you. Be careful how you do—
that girl's all mouth and swallows and I swear
Hell burns the bottom of her throat. Bears
silence well, but that don't mean she hears.
Listen, Flatback Sally got nothing no man needs.
Let a good girl be your vessel: Sally bleeds
for a man to stop her spilling. You should know
when girls like Sally bleed, it's all for show.
What smile she shows, there's twice that grimace hid,
her porchlight eyes like lures. Believe me, kid—
Sally may look purty there, beneath you, on her back.
Like moonlight on steel teeth. A new-laid trap.

Type

1.

The women huddled outside One-Eyed Jacks, taking nips
of cheap whiskey secreted inside their trunks, a savings
when it takes a pint to get you there, though at five or six
I wasn't sure where they were trying to go, but leaving
that, I knew I wanted to go with them. I cherried my lips
red with Lifesavers and smoked crayons, watched them giving
themselves to ugly men against the alleyway wall, the bricks
I ran my hands over the next day, listening, even believing
they might tell me how to hold a woman, how to kiss
her like an ugly man, but better, so she felt I was saving
her from a lifetime of ugly men with their spitting dip
and rotting teeth, their hands filthy with a kind of living
I didn't want to understand, but wanted to imitate well
enough to touch a woman in a way that might send me to Hell.

2.

The first time I touch a woman (in a way that might send me to Hell
the way some see) I wash her feet. A ceremony at church, it's
reminiscent of Christ at the Last Supper. Desire swells
like fear inside my chest. While I kneel before her, she sits,
looking down at me from perfect righteousness. I know how Adam fell
from Grace: he tasted what a woman gave him. Her foot fits
perfectly inside my teenage hand. I vibrate for her like a rung bell.
A song fills the space between us: "Just As I Am." The candles, lit
beside Communion bread. "Just As I Am," dear God, I want to tell

You how I feel for You is how I feel for her, love or snake-bit
or something else terrifying. I repent. Her soft skin smells
like cherry blossoms. What if? dear God, what if I don't repent?
More than anything, I long to feel safe. To know You. To understand.
Want, more than anything, peace. But her skin. My trembling hand.

3.

I want, more than anything, peace. Her skin beneath my trembling hand
is rougher than my skin. I first saw her chain-smoking outside work.
All day I watched her run from station to station. Watched and planned,
along with half the men. She wasn't beautiful, but she had a look.
Something shone from within her like a light. She swept the sand
from the factory floor like a woman waiting for deliverance. Perks
of physical labor, I guess. Sometimes she would tuck a wild strand
of hair behind her ear, and I'd know: I wanted her, whatever it took,
whatever I had to be, or give, or do. If I had to pretend
to admire the well-muscled men. If I had to screw, or sing, or drink
like I never worried a day. I forgot to worry if I sinned.
She'd chain-smoke in bed. I'd read aloud from a good book.
We made love the way she worked: frenzied and alone inside
ourselves. When she left in the morning, I bowed my head and cried.

Drive

Mirror. A cracked-dirt patch
of mirror shards. A man
who calls his dirt a yard,
who calls his woman *mine*. Wine-
dark with fury beneath the rag
of his undershirt, stiff beneath
the knotted pride of his spine.
On a scale from one to ten,
his pain level is *fine*. On a scale
from one to *this is my last beer*,
he's nearly back to black sleep,
having passed her fear some hours past.
She's thin in the window like a blade
of grass, edged like a glass flask
her cognac lips the stopper of her
eyes. If a kindly older man was to drive by
in a rattletrap of an old truck, he'd cast
his eyes out quick, then bring them back.
He'd pride himself on *minding his own*,
and he'd head home. But later, when
he looked in the mirror, he'd know.
Though he might not tell himself out loud.
A man don't just fall asleep that way,
in the sharp glass dirt of his own yard.
No sane woman has eyes that hard.

Sally Considers Taking the Train Away

Behind its whistle, the train gathers
her gaze, skipping like a pebble

toward anyplace else. (As if *away*
was a place she might belong.

As if *away* was a song.)

Sally's eyes desired
a city full of men

to pocket their cries like afterthoughts.

In the city no man loves
you like a country

man loves you, with cold hands
roughened by early work.

What woman needs it anyway?

that particular gentleness
men save for mornings after

fields? City: a proliferation of eyes,
unmet. City: a nakedness.

Strutting around like god
knows who might see.

House Soon to Catch Fire

Upstairs, a man
with swarming wasps for eyes

paces the carpet bare.
Bent birdcage of a woman downstairs.

Falling matchstick of a man
who only wants to rise

like song, like the blush of pride
in his children's cheeks.

Brief fever dream of a man
whose senses whisper lies.

What gift can he offer
his children? His name,

that prison cell inside his neighbors' glares?
The desperate shame

of broken teeth, of ugliness
that can't afford disguise? That man

looks at his wife, sees only bars.
Listens for birdsong, hears broken cars.

Such a man would maybe
trade a match for unheard blame,

would settle for ash lifted skyward on a flame.

Two

Song

A woman alone in the boat of a man.
A woman a moan in the throat of a man.
Brief stone afloat in the moat of a man.
Secret sewn into the coat of a man. Note

a man, how he struts down the road of a girl.
How his rough voice cuts the ode of a girl.
What's she owed? Not the world he's made
of her fear. Not the shade of him here where

she's paid with her tears. *End the game.* So
she thinks, as she drinks one more beer.
End the game! Yes, but thinks: who will pay
for the child? Make a way for the child?

How she prays for that child! So wild.
The dirt on her knees is a cry for a life
where to live will mean more than to die.
Goodbye is the bone in the throat of her now,

a huge stone sinking the boat of her now,
while she stands in the bow, child in hand,
singing the last mournful note of her now.

Stripper

Whatever you think you know of me is wrong.
I came up in church. I remember all the songs—
"Amazing Grace." "Just As I Am." "For All the Saints."
I spent a lifetime being what I ain't.
I spent my childhood on a desperate man.
He spent himself against me. Now, I can
touch a man without him touching back.
I'm real good, too. I got the knack
for making an invisible man feel seen.
That's why they come, you know? They clean
their dirty fingernails and shave up neat,
and sit there still as Sunday under me.
Just as they are, so wonderfully unmade.
I'm the patron saint of getting paid
for less than what a man will sometimes steal.
Sundays, I repent. It's a good deal.

Magical Thinking

In November of my 40th year, I began to believe
there was meaning everywhere. It started with marbles

leaching their sparkling ways up from beneath the lawn,
orange and red glinting in the sun, and me, needing

desperately something to mean. Those marbles
had worked back from burial. It was a message

from God: *Nothing is hidden that will not be disclosed.*
Did that mean the time I let a boy kiss me against

his Camaro, guide my hand to something I couldn't
yet understand? The heat from his car burning my skin.

Some girls don't come easy to grace, and I was one,
skipping through every wildness I came across. God

in me like a chipped tooth I couldn't stop tonguing,
couldn't stop cutting myself against. I wanted to be

fixed. Fixed, or left alone to push a girl against a car
and kiss her while she sparkled like glass in the sun.

Sinners Anonymous

A woman kneels in the dark barn.

In the ditch before the church, hard rain washes
dye from a handful of hair.

In the basement of the church, eyes
require a girl's surrender.

What are you sorry for? asks the preacher
of the silence, and from the silence

her silence returns.
My name is Sally, and I'm

addicted to mercy (hi, Sally)
looking for a deal worth kneeling for.

A woman kneels before
what makes her sorry: silence

where a girl wants sobs. Hard rain
washes the bullshit from her boots.

The preacher polishes empty pews.
Eyes polish a woman's shame:

twenty bucks will get you
all the heat you can handle.

Tell us, girl: what are you sorry for?

Birthright

Fear will make a man
lie about how he loves you

and Sally knows just how to scare a man.
(Beneath her summer clothes,

her belly swells. A song,
sudden as dark, overtakes the day.)

Mercy wells up inside her
like the flood a girl becomes

in the basement of a cruel man's need.
Fear will make a woman

dream of another country,
the motherland a woman can become.

Sally dreams vast fields of desperate eyes.
Hope: a mother will never be left

alone with a dangerous dream.
Mercy: a daughter

born to cut glances from men.

Mother

I'm not ashamed of anything I have or haven't done.
Not that it's your business, or anybody's, really. Though
it's nothing the whole county don't already know.
I have four daughters. A son. A different daddy
for each one. And every one of them pays me. I'm no fool.
The other parents bring their kids to school, and to
games and playdates. I hear the things they say.
Listen: I've been stuck in this town, in this life,
in this name and all the names they name me,
I've been stuck being the person they believed
since I was just a child. Just a *pregnant* child.
Who are they? They're nothing but a bunch of mice
the cat didn't catch. When have they ever talked
about how I do my job, pay my bills, how I own
my little house outright? I've never had the chance
to follow myself along a winding path that led me
to a place I knew was mine. With five kids? I've just
never had the time. So I work, at a place they all know,
so I drink, at a place they all know, so I live, in a place
they all know, with my children and our different names.
So sometimes I have a visitor; it's my house. A man
and his rough touch can become, for a while, a path
that leads somewhere new. Sometimes, a man can
be another place to live, for a moment, for a person
who will never leave. What credit do I get for never
leaving? When was my story no longer mine to tell?

Park

Almost pretty: the sun glinting off broken
glass. Almost a place where a child should
play. It's almost August. What is August?

A trash bag filled with clinking bottles.
What is this place if it isn't drunk by noon?
Children will gather anywhere. Around

anybody with a story to tell of another
place, of how to go. Almost pretty
enough, this place. Almost cool enough

to breathe. The women pushing strollers
are almost to term again. The sweat stains
through their shirt backs. One has a toddler

who lives in the corner of her vision, who
she only moves toward as if he is a threat.
Gathering tiny bits of glass in his fat fists.

It's almost pretty. The deft dance of her hands.
Stay with me, the mother says, and he knows
he will, in the same way he knows her name

is Mama. Her name might as well be Mama.
What is August but some heavy thing
to be carried in the heat? This place

but the poor fit of a wrong name?
A mother. A long pull on a cold beer.
If this place was ever part of a picture,

it must have been almost beautiful. It must
have been the frame that broke. Little hands
burying in glass in glass all the secret things

they know they know.

Woman

The way a charming man can ride his violence
to any height, I decide to speak the truth
is worth all the long years I kept my silence

like a right I wasn't sure I even wanted.
(Like a rite my body tried to stop performing.)
The way a man can ride a lie (so flaunted!)

to truth inside another woman's need.
(I couldn't be the truth inside his lie.)
Truth became in me a kind of greed

leaving me gasping after it, like air.
(Your mouth, pressed to mine, only sought
instead of giving.) I breathed in fear

your lie would choke the flower of truth I knew.
And every garden I planted would grow for you.

Knock Knock

Who's there? Nobody. Nobody who? Nobody

unfolding a list of kind words. Nobody who knows you
need them. Nobody who wouldn't save you

for later, for a famine, who won't someday feed you
to his own need. How is a joke like a woman's

breast? It's a feast for a thousand eyes. Sometimes
it falls flat under its own weight. Hangs there, full

of guilt and nourishing the next nobody. Who wouldn't
lift a nipple to his lips? What a woman knows of feeding

is what a lamb knows of a knife: nothing, then sudden teeth.
When you're dinner, everything looks

like a mouth: your front door, dark throat
of your own hall, white picket fence like a jaw

closing toward you. When you're a joke, everything
sounds like a laugh. Even your pleading. Even

your own desperate knocking at your neighbor's door.

Grandmother

I cried my eyes sore worrying over that girl,
coming home all hours of the night. I know
them boys. They'll look for all the world
like something worth a life. *All show
and no go,* my own Mama always said.
Sometimes I look at her and feel this fear
opening inside me like a mouth. That dread
like a warning only a woman can hear.
What if that girl never gets out of this place?
I know them boys. I married one of my own.
Nice enough. Smart enough. An honest face.
From here, o'course. I've always known
he was the homeplace being built for me.
Home enough. Life enough. You see?

Sally Teaches Mercy Best She Knows

Mercy was a lonely road
between two silent fields

dead-ending in a town of growing glares.

She grew like a smile
salting a thousand sneers

She grew like a silence
calling a woman to song.

Sally lost and found another man.

Plenty forgot their names,
if plenty had known

their names, that crumbling cabin
they kept at the edge of need.

More than once, Sally found Mercy
on her knees beside the bed,

begging the good Lord for one good man.
Mercy, said Sally, you get the love you deserve.

Daughter

How did I come here? I followed a man.
Tanned, taut rope of a man. All my hope
on a man. Packed my bags and left home
without a ghost of a plan. Some man!
Gone now, same way my mother ran.
My mother, who, one morning, packed
her toothbrush and a dull knife
and everything she ever tried
to tell me, and followed a ghost of a man right
out of my life. My mother, who had a heart
like a catcher's mitt. The one thing we had
in common the desperate need to be called
wife. Mommy, too, maybe, but always
first: wife. I used to tell her what I'd never be,
which was generally anything she was. More
fool me! She last saw her mother get on a bus.
I'm different, though, now. I'm teaching my
daughter how to pick the right man. Sometimes,
when I trace the veins of her sleeping hand,
I can still hear my mother say: *darling,*
we're all clichés. A cliché is something
so true that every word you don't say
needs at least three others. Here's a *cliché*:
The only thing we have in common
is everything. We both hoped I'd turn out
better than my mother.

Three

Shadows

There is another town beneath this town,
where secret drinkers sneak to buy their pints
and secret lovers sneak to make their love
while sleepers sleep. I wake again to you.
There is another want beneath this want,

that doesn't fear to touch, or to lie down
beside you, skin to skin. Oh, town that haunts
the town you see, like fog hanging above
a quiet street. (A lie cannot be true.)
The truth I know: your body is a taunt

I struggle to ignore. Your silk nightgown
wants my hands (the truth wants what it wants).
The hands beneath my hands are shadowed gloves.
The town beneath the town is moonlit blue.
The lie we speak covers the truth we can't.

Crank

For a woman who can't afford teeth,
it's a well to wish in. A different hell
to twist in. A cell to kiss in. Less a pail
to piss in than this promise: you'll never
really care where you piss again.
Machine of a human being who says
If I am a machine, let them have my body.
I will go to live among the clouds.
What is a drug but a cold coin dropped
down the well of a throat? What is a wish
but a castle fashioned from smoke?
What is a tweaker? The unwinding
machine of a woman's jaw, pumping
the rusted pistons of her teeth.
What is crank? Hot glass. A brief sheen.
For a woman who can't afford church,
it's a burnt clean. Crank is the grease
for the newest American dream.
For a woman who can't afford sleep,
it's the newest scheme: cover the hurt
of your work with the hurt of your shame.
Trade your bones for a good buck.
Turn the crank all day, each moment the same.
Get fired for stealing a pop off the lunch truck.

That Saved a Wretch Like Me

Sally stumbles across the nighttime street,
fake fur coat hanging on her frame

like she was wrapped in roadkill. A complete
tragedy in one half-drunken act. Same

old story, like an echo rung through time.
Broken woman, more sung about than singing.

Tellers of stories, carefully crafting rhymes,
might find her haunting. Sad spectacle, bringing

a pint of cinnamon whiskey to her lips
again. A woman left to her own devices

might lose herself, might let her pain eclipse
her peace. Mercy's memory entices

a daughterless mother to sell what she has to sell
and hurl herself headlong into Hell.

Emigrant

Growing up in this town was like eighteen years
of the me I need to be pacing inside the me they think
I am. My body a dank room. My body a tower
with no stairs. My body a silk tightening around whatever
is really me until whatever is me can't fit, can't find
a way to break free. Thirteen minutes after the work
shift I picked up specifically because it was during
graduation ended, I climbed the steps of the first bus
out of town. Played like I was sundown, the dark
a cape I shook out behind me. The dark a gift
I could finally afford. Everything about a small town
is bigger than a fraction of impact. The bus steady
as a predator, sightless through the increasing lack
of light. Like a Great White. Have you ever seen
Shark Week? A shark is unfathomably old, as
far as animals go, is a near-perfect killing machine.
This thing, this shark, must constantly move, or die.
We lived so far away from anything else we couldn't
have *Shark Week*. Until I was in the city, I never saw
such a thing. A shark moves like a bus filled with
people in the night, desperate to be anywhere else.
A shark moves like a person pacing inside tightening
skin. I came back again, of course. I had to come back.
Does anybody ever really leave? I came back on that
same bus, eating its way through the dark, for the only
reason a shark stops swimming: death. Or dying. Not
mine, but somebody who kept me like gravity in her
palm, somebody who taught me how the world slopes

toward home. Sundowning, they call it, the way my
mother swam through the end, the world an ocean
trying to hold her in. Her pacing as if she must die
                                      or shed her skin.

Field

Summer day like a held breath, like held words
in a woman's mouth, like a woman's mouth stopped
by a chafed palm. Day like a chafed palm beneath
a work glove. A work glove hung from electric wire.

Electric wire pulsing above a house. Where there is
a house, there is a straight road beside a house,
and where there's a straight road, there's a road's
end. What does the city know of the road's end?

City a perfumed woman with crossed arms. City
a man faced seaward. City man never needs to think
about roads, and who makes roads, and who makes
his body into roads. Who paves a quiet living over dirt.

What does the road's end know of a knot of streets?
Where every way becomes every other way, every
day leads to another day of chasing a road that never
lets day rest. Country a hard woman, city held to her

breast. Country a woman alone at the end of a way.
Eyes running hard from field to darkling wood,
from wood to the back lawn where her children play.
Here, where a word held home is still thought good.

Here, where a woman's breath makes a summer day.

Factory

South from courthouse square, the church bells ring
time to clock in. A call to partake in the sacrament
of making. Here's a factory, placed in the crease
of a hand. A factory, the promise of daily labor;
here's peace in the land. A factory is a lung,
breathing a people, exhaling a town. In, deeply,
with sweat and lifetime and dreams; out, with
force behind it, order. A factory is the land resting
behind a border, and the border itself. A factory
is a pantry full of stocked shelves. A town is a place
where a person can go to a store and pay a bit
of her life to buy a thing that she made with a
bit of her life, and she can walk away feeling
proud of her life. A town is what happens between
work and church. A life is what happens around
a town. There are men whose hands get lost
on the way to work, end up wandering the paths
of the forest called woman, the desert of a constant
thirst for wine, the grasping vine of a hot pipe.
A factory requires no leap of faith. Repetitive
work is a kind of balm for the open wound
of doubt. The church bells ring the workday out.

Lines Written Between Shifts

Smoke hangs like questions in the break shack's air:
Do you want to die early? Don't you feel that fear
pressing you like a machine? Aren't you wasting
your life with work? The skinny girl says *I'm fasting
again. What did you bring for lunch today?*
You wish you could tell her the secret to joy.
(Is loving what you are more than what you do?)
(Is knowing when you leave here, you're still you?)

In the parked cars, line workers hit their pipes.
One will die from the pills he takes to sleep.
Nobody will remember his given name.
The line will keep running. The press will slam
over and over all day. You'll breathe the dirt.
Break is for questions that can't be asked at work.

Settlement

This town like a raised fist. The clench of it. The industrial sulfur stench of it. Soundtrack running behind a poet dying early. Chinese fingertrap town. This downtown, a nightmare of pulling. This town that eats its own. This town where everybody eventually ends up. Pretending-to-be-purgatory town, but what is the difference between burning away the sin of a soul and burning a soul for sin—simply eternity? Eternal town, each moment like a day of panic blood, the iced frontier of afraid veins. Vein-collapsing vacuum of a town. Mythic boredom town. Town in which the most interesting thing is the roads that lead away. Town waiting at the bottom of everything. Only fifty-four minutes north of a city town. Then left at the post office. This movie poster of a man's shadow standing over a girl town. This silent picture town. Town Where Nobody Becomes Anything, town where everyone becomes something in the mouths of everyone else, everlasting gobstopper town. If you were a person you'd be a bully town. If a god you'd be silent. If you were a movie scene you'd be that one with the idiot kid rapturous over a bag in the wind. We all reuse our Walmart bags town. We all reuse our lovers town. We all kindly refuse your assistance town. We all stand on the courthouse lawn and release balloons town where we never receive letters back. Town where if you're from this town you'll never be a New Yorker town, and if you leave for New York you'll forever lose this town. Hometown team town. Covered cage of a town. Where everything happened and keeps happening. Drone of a beehive town relaxing you to sleep. Town that promises to love you as long as you stay.   Licking pretend honey from your lips.

House Down in the Holler

Where a thin woman wields a straw broom
against a siege of river mud. Shade

of her mother prowling her blood: *just because
you're poor doesn't mean you can't be clean.*

The latest baby hollering in the back bedroom.

If a man comes home
like a storm making landfall against a shore,

his children thin trees bent before his wind,
a mother must be the sun.

In a room with three walls
and a visqueened hole, a mother is home

for a child's fear. Mama, broom in hand,
humping away through black mud, chasing

the fattest river rat you ever saw,
chewing a bite of that latest baby's sole.

The End of the Eggs

We break the last egg for the child,
        though we have four for dinner.
(Hunger coppers the mouth like fear,
        when there isn't more for dinner.)

Desert land where idols swallow
        eyes of men and spit back stones,
you may bless our brothers' deaths,
        but we can't eat war for dinner.

Cage-free? The chickens strut
        the country roads like dumb gods.
Judge our hurries. Snap their skinny necks
        toward us, too poor for dinner.

Stories are like eggs, and truth like yolks.
        (They only show when broken.)
Some bodies are shells, breaking themselves
        empty, too sore for dinner.

Work Song of the Unbroken, Joyfully

Call us alone in the corn kissing, stressing ourselves
like syllables on the young tongues of one another, electric

we strike the endless field of night. Fire of muscle
inside our skins, and bone. Call us fire in the direst sky.

Drawn and borne forth, down the warm street of your breath,
its swift intake against the frost. A boy cannot be found

who has not been lost. Sprung from the trap boys, snapping
our necks in your direction, call us a brawl of boys.

Mythological in the mouths of you. Gathering the world
into the coiled baskets of our eyes, we are seeding the soil

with our teeth. Call us your tongue snaking around
a word you can't say. Sewn into the cheeks of river fish.

Swimming into the caves beneath the creek. Call us
catching dinner with rough hands, springing free the greasefish

fattening the silted bottoms of our days. Don't be a hero
boys, we are workaday tattoos, stamped ourselves

into leather and wore ourselves smooth. Braided sinew
of everything we've killed. The almost-chewed. Flattened

for flat's sake, feeding ourselves in pieces to machines.
Dire in the fired kilns of ourselves. We are lowborn

in our own countries. Dust-flung from the God-flesh.
We are tied to the spined jiggers of our years.

Beautifully spent in our skinlessness. Name us alive
in the choke of a potent-throated God, our backs muscled

triumphant beneath the goad. Here, where every boy
is a working dead boy, where every dead boy

is a dead boy and nothing more.

Consider the Trigger

The difference between winter
and winter without, that deep
freezer humming like a beast.

What hunger sleeps in your belly,
Girl? What fear? This end of year
is colder than the last, this fast

approaching fast, these short
days long. We can't afford to eat
if killing's wrong. Consider this

a warning shot. Or not.
Our children are not trees, to take
their life from light, and anyway

there's almost none. This meat
our sun, this lifeblood you disdain,
this loss of life our living's gain.

Meat for bones and straining backs,
double shifts and chopped woodstacks.
Meat for making all we do. Meat

for shipping it to you.

Tommy Two Fingers Quits His Job

You know the store already counts the cost
of any limbs get lost to them machines?
Think o'that! All your gadgets, desperate dreams
priced right in. Since I only lost
the two least fingers on my weaker hand
(thank the good Lord, I can still strum strings)
I got a little less. But I got plans.
I ain't just gonna spend this. I got things
I wanna do, now I'm redneck rich.
First, I'm buying teeth, a full, straight smile.
Second, I'll pay off that son of a bitch
married to my mother. Then awhile
on the road. I'm actually a decent singer.
Think o'that! Just 'cause I lost a couple fingers.

Even the Road Away Leads Sally Home

Sally took the road that led away
from Mercy, that cell

an empty home that held her.
She meant to claim herself

a name anew. Meant
to retake her *me* from every *you*.

(You, a sneer, a fear,
as yet unformed. You: unmet

desire, as yet unborn.)
Mercy took the road that led away

from Sally, that night
the empty crib that held her.

(You: a flash of light,
a wickedness. You: a girl,

a daughter, axe-
blade that felled her.)

Four

Mercy, Defined

Mercy was a girl grown
wise to the world's lies

winter whipping her back like a testament

to youth, that early fervor
no girl survives.

Mercy shaved a pork bone
down to a fine point, used it

to pick the gristle from her teeth.

What is a world?
Another set of hands pawing a girl.

What is a girl?
A mouth like a sprung trap.

Kid

The thing about living here: even a child can know things. I know every shortcut, every bike path through the park, every street between every house. I know every kid who lives in each one. Every crack in every sidewalk that can possibly catch a toe or a skateboard or bike. Who is cousins with who. Whose parents the police don't like. Whose parents the *priests* don't like. I'm kinda kidding, but not really, you know? It's like that. Kids know more than adults, anyway, and in a small town, *everybody* talks. I know where Spring comes to the park first, and when, and how. (In the back part, behind a certain tree, a small patch of lenten roses. Mr. Hower, the older man who cuts the grass, planted them. To remember his wife. You know.) Living here, a kid knows things he shouldn't know. He can go anywhere, because he has a town full of adults who are sure he's being watched by other adults. And he is, but a kid learns how to blend in. A kid learns early that adults will never really see us unless they believe we're not safe. And they believe this town itself is safe. So here we are, kids, standing outside the window where Mrs. So-and-So cleans the kitchen in her skimpy underwear. Here we are, on the corner, planning a fight. Kids are behind the liquor store, sipping cheap wine and kids are in your bedroom drawer stealing joints. Because we know every house where the parents hold drugs. A small town is a place where everybody watches out for everyone else so they have something to say

Monday at work. A place where each person knows
the name of every other person's kid, but rarely knows exactly where
his is. A small town is more seduction than truth, like a trick
coin in the hand of a con. Please don't tell any of this to my Mom.

Farmer

Save your sorry. Your sorry won't get me
my crops in before the frost. Your sorry

won't fill the propane tank. Confess me up
a big old sack of free feed, while you're at it.

What I don't need? A man who can't outpace
his sorries, who leads 'em around like a pack

of fair-weather friends. Another man hog-tied
by shoulda done. I knew a man once, he plowed

through each day like sorries leaded his boots,
each foot dragging the bodies of his regrets.

His whole life was an apology. God, what
did he think? It would stop him dying? He died,

like we all do: with dry lips and not enough
to drink. Sorry is death for no reason. Sorry

is men dying everywhere except the spot
where you stand, and you laying yourself

down in the sand. Each death deserves a life.
It's like, I don't know. Here! It's like a field.

The most fertile field needs a fallow year.
The man who never rests his field grows

nothing but the knowledge of should
have done. What should I have done?

My son was just learning how to run the big
plow, and if he was too young, if another year

would have kept him from its blades—what
should I have done? What will it help

to plant, again and again, that field where
my boy died, and to harvest regret from

the black soil of the past? Don't tell me
you're sorry, I used to tell him when he

messed up, it doesn't fix it. Don't tell me
you're sorry. Just stop doing the wrong thing.

Boy

City boy don't know fear like a country boy knows
fear. That nowhere road through tall corn. Home
a house he can't see from here. House like a closed
eye. House like a beautiful woman who never needed
him. Like a strange man's wall of cheap cologne.
House as forever away as a field's end. House like
a false friend. What does a city boy know of a dead
end? Of living there? Of something rustling the corn
maybe ten rows in, of the lift of every tiny hair?
Fear, that animal cry too suddenly close. Broken
surface of the dark pond. Fear like a frayed bond.
City boy, what you know of a last name that chokes you
like a rope? What you know of slow death by no hope?
Of entombment in the sweetest words. What does
the city know of sick herds? Of work that starts
before a man can think? City knows: them country
boys, they drink. They drink, and smoke, or chew,
and go to church. City don't know country. How
we work. How we laugh and cry and dance and
love and scheme. City don't know how quiet can
grow fear. City don't care what a country boy dreams.
City don't listen.   It will never be city here.

Wanderer

I want to own what little I own
outright. Y'know? Not owe
tomorrow's work today. This way

I'm lighter than what holds me here.
Don't get me wrong. I plan to stay.
This little town's as good as any other.

But I'm the kind of man needs an escape.
A running truck, a woman I won't mind
bidding goodbye to in the rearview mirror.

Want a steady man? Try my brother.
He was always hungry more than anything.
There's not a credit card he hasn't signed.

Here I am, for now. This shithole town.
Home's wherever money weighs you down.

Old Maid

Some women collect goodbyes from lying men.
Babies they can't afford. Sin heaped on sin.
I myself have books and time to read.

Don't you dare look down at me that way.
I decided long ago, the roles a woman plays
to keep a man, I wouldn't play. I don't need

for any material thing. Some women's lives
are twisted unrecognizable, like knives
once used to pry at padlocks. I was freed

from all the lies life would have asked of me.
A woman's life's a river, a man's a stone.
Sink or float, I'll carry on alone.

Preacher

None of my classes prepared me for the omnipresence
of manure. Manure as an irrefutable force. No, no, I kid.
Of course I kid. God loves us all the same. Am I right?

It wasn't my first choice, of course, but even a servant
of God has to start somewhere. Even Jacob had a ladder
he had to climb. Am I right? I kid! It's just—you won't

think me proud? It's just, they told me as seminaries go,
it was the best. The newest thoughts, the biggest names
in the business. Well, except, of course, that is, for God.

I kid! We all face our own trials. I told myself, relax,
in a town this size, every road leads to the highway,
and every highway leads eventually home. To the city,

paved in gold. If I'm being honest, though, I've gotten lost
so many times here—on country roads, on hardpack dirt, on
barely-there lakefront lanes. I've gotten so lost I had to take

the highway on faith. I've gotten so lost I couldn't tell
which lightened sky was home. We face our own trials.
In a small congregation, each person carries more

of each person toward the Lord. And everybody can
seem so damn sure! It's like they expect me to know
exactly what's right, and exactly which road leads

to the narrow way. Yes, I was first in my class at the top-
ranked school, and yes, I read the newest arguments.
But everything here is so goddamned black and white.

I'm sorry. I never use that word. I'm so sorry. It comes
to this: we both want something the other cannot give.
In the city, there are a thousand short streets off the

freeway, and a thousand ways to get to the same place.
And nobody expects you to lead them there. Am I right?

Liquor Store Clerk

Here she come, old Sally, needing
her nightly nips o' whiskey, always
the cheapest kind we carry, cinnamon.
That expression like a bad alibi.
Death was still waiting to happen
to her then. You could see it coming,
though, like something chasing after
her, a shadow cast in the dark rooms
of her eyes. Who was I to judge her
for them few nips? I sold hard lives
a softness. A measure o' peace.
Preacher says nobody's saved
after ten minutes anyway.

The Grand Dragon of the KKK
Is Buried Near My House

They let him down, four local boys
with faces valleyed by years,
and eyes that skitch away sideways
like outdoor dogs. *He'd never miss a piece
o' blueberry pie* says the one, agreement
hanging between them like long years,
like all the black mornings through which
they'd staggered home, drunk as a man could get
if he drank from overtime to closing time.
They are men in various stages of falling down.
They lower him home, and it's a good thing
he died young, thinks at least one,
*my strength ain't what it once was,
I don't know how much longer I'll hold up.*
He was somethin' says the guy
whose shoulder hurts worst, *remember
the summer we was all on tv?* and he lifts his eyes
upward toward memory: himself at 19,
his muscles coiled ready inside his skin.
He really was a man to be reckoned with.
Nobody says nothing, but they're all agreeing,
rubbing the young back into their joints,
his name like a balm that burns away the years.
And again, as if somebody had disagreed:
*His name means something here, everybody
knowed him for somebody*, and they lift

their eyes again, to bodies before pain,
to the value of a name, here, where every
grave is a pauper's grave, off this nowhere
road, where every car is a car from here.

Soldier

Everybody keep talking about war like they
know war. Like war's they friend, they family,
closer than blood. Come on in, pull up a piece
of fake hardwood floor, and warm you by
the fire. Bring them kiddos, too. Trust us,
we don't mind the more the merrier we count
success by each guest we serve. Everybody
keep talking about war like war is a sweet dog
who lives somewhere in the neighborhood.
You hunker down in the street when you see
'im you maybe toss him a treat. He's a good
dog just don't wanna be owned. Everybody
call 'im by a different name and 'e goes where
'e goes. And war *is* that. But anybody who ever
loved him a dog knows this: a dog who don't
wanna be owned is a dog you can't trust with
your children. War comes to your door sometime
pantin' like 'e thirsty, and you turn toward
the kitchen sink. His eyes laughin' behind you
all the time. War the type to pad right up close
to anything you own and dance away down
the street with your meat in 'is teeth. War
is more than a sweet li'l puppy scrounging
for scraps; war is a dog who knows what
'e needs cuz 'e knows what 'e's never had, he
knows any night he might have to go without.
And your child's hand rests in his gentle jaws.

Seeing Too Much Is Seeing Nothing

A woman stands at the sink, training
her eyes on the following day

and missing
the girl following her around.

Mercy's saving all her faith for silences
these days. Summer

mornings in Indiana
are a lie that'll catch you out later.

An unanswered question,
a shame that'll soak your clothes.

What happened to Mercy? a truth
you don't know how to say

is the same as a truth you don't know.
One more little girl

who couldn't be saved. Mercy
split the county-line crick

and walked through on dry ground.
Sally swore she never saw the day.

As for me and my house, we will

    praise the Lord of porkfat and Flatback Sally
        fat arms thrust elbow-deep in dirt.
praise hurt   grippin' your back like an accolade
       praise staid   men, scotch and gin,
the same sin again and again   lives measured
      in overtime and ass   praise sass
praise heat   praise good weeks affording meat
      as for me and my house *we* will praise
bluegrass and tired women who raise   their hands
     and hell   and any children they might make
women who take   a man's attention
     and dance just like they work
(all fits and jerks)   (to kill a hunger)
      praise hunger   that syncopated song
that drives our beat   praise hunger
     the only word we never eat
(dark animals slung low against the wood
     slink along at every shadow's end)
praise good killing   one's own dinner and the skin
     tearing free from muscle at our hands
praise desperate land   and our own planted plans
     the crackle on our tongues of recipes
we wrote   praise lard and hard throats
     stopped forever against frivolous weeping
and Sunday sleeping   as for me and my house
     we will serve   seven good men

for every meal   potatoes cooked
      seven different ways   and call it praise
our best days our hardest days
          our best days our longest days

Acknowledgments

The American Journal of Poetry: "Crank," "Mother," "Settlement," "Soldier"

Antigonish Review: "Bait"

Anti-Heroin Chic: "House Down in the Holler," "Park"

Atticus Review: "Sally Considers Taking the Train Away"

B O D Y: "Boat," "Song"

Chiron Review: "Mercy, Defined," "The Old Man Warns the Young Man at the Bar"

Journal of Applied Poetics: "Bar," "Daughter," "Drive"

One Art: "Factory," "Farmer," "Fire," "House Soon to Catch Fire," "Inheritance," "Lines Written Between Shifts," "Shadows," "Sinners Anonymous," "Stripper," "Type"

OPEN: Journal of Arts & Letters: "Emigrant," "Mercy, Indiana"

Passengers Journal: "Magical Thinking"

Rattle: "The Grand Dragon of the KKK Is Buried Near My House," "Kid"

2River: "Sally Teaches Mercy Best She Knows," "Seeing Too Much Is Seeing Nothing"

Valparaiso Poetry Review: "Woman"

Verse-Virtual: "Grandmother," "Property," "Wanderer"

Writers Resist: "History"

Thank you to my parents, Mary and Joe Custer for their unconditional love; to Francesca Bell for her endless support and friendship; to Diane Lockward, who took a chance on this book; to Joe Chaney, whose belief always made me believe; and to the many poets and readers who have read and supported this work.

And a very special thanks to an NEA fellowship for the twin gifts of time and financial support, both of which allowed me to write most of the poems in this collection.

About the Author

Rachel Custer is the author of *The Temple She Became* (Five Oaks Press, 2017). She is the recipient of a 2019 fellowship from the National Endowment of the Arts and a 2015 mentorship from the Association of Writers and Writing Programs. Her poetry has appeared in numerous journals, including *Rattle, OSU: The Journal, B O D Y, The American Journal of Poetry, The Antigonish Review,* and *Open: Journal of Arts & Letters.* She attended the University of Indiana and the University of Chicago. She lives in Indiana.

www.rachelcuster.wordpress.com